W9-BCB-175

Love Surrealist Poems

Edited by Mary Ann Caws

The University of Chicago Press

Acknowledgements
My warmest thanks to Jennifer Mundy
and to Mary Richards for their inspired
suggestions about this volume, a most
engaging project to work on from start to
finish. Long live surrealism, and love too.
Mary Ann Caws, August 2001

Published by Tate Publishing, a division
of Tate Enterprises Ltd, Millbank, London
SW1P 4RG and The University of Chicago
Press, Chicago 60637

ISBN 0-226-09871-0 (cloth)

CIP data is available.

Designed and typeset by Anne Odling-Smee
at August
Printed by Snoeck-Ducaju & Zoon, Gent,
Belgium

Contents

The poetics of surrealist love

Rage and mad love

In the beginning was an initial, inspiring rage: down with everything bourgeois, everything to do with the dull past. Surrealism sprang up in opposition to logic, the fundamental principle of bourgeois thinking characteristic of those whom the nineteenth-century poet Arthur Rimbaud, beloved by the surrealists, called *les assis* – 'the seated ones'. Whether standing or lying down – whatever position the highly charged erotics of the surrealist encounter and union chooses to assume – surrealism is always vital, enlivening and intensifying.

Although based in France, surrealism was an international movement, guaranteeing a continuous circulation of ideas, attitudes, styles and substance. It had its origins in the dada movement, founded in Zurich in 1915. The dadaists greatly enjoyed undoing every idea of the rational in favour of the violently active and highly coloured. Their performances included simultaneous readings of the same text in different languages, and combined outlandish costume with gesture, noise, art and drama. The French poets André Breton and Louis Aragon were involved in the Paris dada group, alongside the Romanian Tristan Tzara, in the early 1920s. By 1923, however, dada gave way to the more ordered manifestations of the surrealist group, which published its first manifesto a year later. Surrealism began as a literary movement, visual art only being fully accepted when Breton later acknowledged that 'vision is the most powerful of the senses', and downplayed the aural: 'Let the curtain fall on the orchestra.'

Surrealism's heroic period was in the 1920s and the 1930s, years marked by intense exploration of the lower levels of the psyche, by the invention of new types and techniques of making art and by the publication of volumes of love poetry and meditations on madness and its connection with genius and love. High points include Paul Eluard's *In the Absence of Silence* (*Au défaut du silence*) of 1925, Breton's poetic essay/novel *Nadja*, published in 1928, the collaborative text *Immaculate Conception* (*L'Immaculée Conception*), and Breton's collection of love poems, *The Air of Water* (*L'Air de l'eau*) of 1934.

During the Second World War, Breton went into exile, moving to New York with his second wife Jacqueline Lamba and their daughter Aube. The painters Max Ernst and André Masson also fled to the States, while Aragon, Eluard and Tzara remained in Europe, secretly circulating their resistance writings. The great surrealist love poet Robert Desnos was to die of typhoid fever in the concentration camp of Terezina in 1945. In New York the surrealist games and writings continued with a temporary collaboration between the surrealists in exile and the New York artists and writers gathered around the journal *View*, edited by Charles-Henri Ford. The surrealist journal *VVV* also dates from this period. On Breton's return to France in 1947, the atmosphere had changed, and the movement changed with it, but what remained was the surrealist view of a gloriously 'mad love': mad, because passionate, beyond all the limits of reason.

From David Gascoyne in England to Aimé and Suzanne Césaire in Martinique, to Léon-Gontran Damas and René Ménil in Guyana, both of whom wrote for the surrealist journal *Tropiques*, and more recently to Octavio Paz in Mexico, surrealist poetry spread far, wide and brilliantly. Surrealists in Paris, such as Gilbert Lély and Joyce Mansour – the latter remarkable for her rabid and revolutionary 'Cries' (*Cris*) of 1953, and 'Tearings' (*Déchirures*) of 1955 – continued the movement, along with Michel Leiris and Julien Gracq, and the magnificently ferocious texts of Annie Le Brun and Radovan Ivsic. Surrealism's poetic and philosophic legacy is everywhere, in the English language as in the French and other European manifestations. Of all modern movements in the combined visual and verbal arts, its heritage is proving to be the most powerful and the most lasting.

Surrealist love poetry

Surrealism laid great stress on the liberating power of sexuality, which found a firm support in the texts of Sigmund Freud. Breton's text 'Mad Love' (*L'Amour fou*), published in 1937, illustrates how for Freud, sexual love 'breaks the collective links created by race, rises above national differences and social hierarchies'. But what mostly mattered to the surrealists was freedom itself. 'Hands off Love!' ran the title of one of the most famous surrealist tracts, written in 1927 and defending Charlie Chaplin's womanising behaviour in the light of the surrealists' ideal of free love. For the French surrealists, the desire for freedom linked the surrealist revolution with the French Revolution two centuries before. Indeed, what remained from dada in surrealism was the spirit of energy and revolution, embodied in Breton's tract of 1923, 'Drop Everything!' (*Lâchez tout!*).

Surrealism carries this energy into a notion of movement. Tzara's notes on art and poetry of 1917 picture the poetic text – and by extension, the painted or sculpted work – rushing down the mountainside, shrieking its joy, putting a quick end to what he designated as the slow-moving ethics of previous morality-based movements, sticky and heavy like chocolate dribbling through human veins. The energetic charge comes from the irrational violence of intensely opposed elements striking with a loud flash and clash. The cubist poet Pierre Reverdy had advocated as early as 1913 an aesthetic of contradictory convergence, in which elements from fields as far opposed as possible would meet, causing a mental explosion. Breton was to base the surrealist aesthetic on this idea of the dramatic mingling of contraries: man and woman, death and life, and so on.

A good part of the erotic excitement provided by surrealist love texts depends on the provocative power of this encounter, recalling the surrealist game 'the one in the other', in which each element is made more interesting by the complexity of the union. From Breton's 'Mad Love', with its union of two bodies, minds and dreams, to the dada-inspired genre of collage, mingling disparate elements, the most highly valued element of surrealism is the dramatic encounter of contraries. And philosophically, psychologically and textually, it is at the very basis of the surrealist love poem.

The surrealist stroller, just out for a walk, typically meets an impossibly haunting, possibly mad, beloved in a street-corner encounter, where opposites come together in the atmosphere of the marvellous. The encounter is sufficient to nourish an entire lifetime of obsessive imagination. The erotics of the meeting depends on both the slightly mad aspect of the one discovered (whose discovery the will itself is responsible for), and the determined surrealist imaginer. Nadja, the woman whom Breton encountered and briefly loved, inspiring his novel of the same name, was mad and finally taken to an asylum, but not before having implicitly accused him of bourgeois behaviour. She had proposed when they were driving together in a car that they should both cover their eyes and drive blindly ahead. Breton admitted: 'I was perhaps not up to what she proposed.' Perhaps not indeed, but then few would have been. Breton was afraid of a love too mad. What remains is the extraordinary journal of the encounter and of the experience of a failed love.

Breton's involvement with Nadja prepared him for the intensity of his passion for Suzanne Muzard, the unidentified 'X' extolled at the end of the book. Flamboyant affairs characterised the lives of the surrealists. Paul Eluard, for example, was first married to the Russian beauty Gala, who for a period was also the lover of the painter Max Ernst before she famously teamed up with the Spanish surrealist Salvador Dalí. Eluard next became half of an emblematically elegant surrealist couple whose other half was the athletic, lovely and fragile Nusch. Her early death in 1946 led to some of his most moving poetry: 'Time Spills Over' (*Le Temps déborde*). The vagaries and tragedies of real life, the heights and plunges of its involved intensities, inspired much surrealist love poetry. Beyond the biographical facts of the poets' experience, however, there was a shared utopian vision among the writers of the group about what love might be, should be, will someday be.

Among all the great love poets of the heroic period of surrealism, Robert Desnos incarnates with the most intricate subtlety the joyously painful play of contraries. His poem 'If You Knew', about distance and presence, is a prime example. His most celebrated prose work incarnates the performance of the play of contraries within its own form. For in 'Freedom or Love!' (*La liberté ou l'amour!*), the juxtaposed terms of the title are either alternatives, placed in opposition, or equivalents, or both. '*L'amour*' sounds like '*la mort*' (death), but in any case, love triumphs over death in the eroticising verbal and conceptual play of notions. The book's heroine, Louise Lame (recalling the word *lame* or knife blade, and at the same time, the soul, *l'âme*), is naked under her leopard-skin coat, as she flees an amorous pursuer. This simultaneous reference to clothing and nakedness is echoed in the double-edged language: 'And now I find you once more just when I thought I had fled you'. Even as she flees, she is a constant presence; even as the pursuer/lover suffers, he is joyous in his suffering.

This is, as we know, the true meaning of passion. Surrealist love picks up on the tradition of courtly love, with all its inbred contraries: to possess is no longer to love, so the truest love is in the pursuit itself. Much of surrealist love poetry is based precisely on this form of contrariness with its permanent arousal of what endlessly remains joyously and necessarily unsatisfied. Love is, and must remain, pursuit. But what differentiates the surrealist vision of love from the courtly love of medieval Provençal poets is the marvellous possibility that an end can be reached, a love consummated, while the vitalising desire for that end, for the consummation, continues. Accomplishment seals nothing off in the universe of surrealism. Everything leads to the next time, which is, as in the opening line of one of Breton's poems included here, 'Always for the first time'.

Surrealism is a therefore a movement of high optimism, and the headiness of mad love is the founding tenet of its poetry. As Breton puts it, this is where 'the attained and the desire no longer exclude one another'. Eluard phrased it as 'desire remaining desire' (*le désir demeuré désir*). Mind, body and spirit are oriented towards the future; anticipatory excitement, the ability to remain in a state of expectation and openness to chance (*disponibilité*) – is the *sine qua non* of surrealist poetic experience. And the intensity of love must remain at white-hot pitch, with all its passion and pain.

The notion of opposition is also implicit in Breton's definition of *convulsive beauty*. As he conceives it, that beauty depends on the reciprocal relations linking the object seen in motion and in repose: 'the word "convulsive", which I use to describe the only beauty that should concern us, would lose any meaning in my eyes were it to be conceived in motion and not at the exact expiration of this motion'. The perfect image of such beauty is 'a speeding locomotive abandoned for years to the delirium of a virgin forest'. This definition is rendered delirious by the dizzying potential of oppositions: motion and rest, speed and halting, the phallic thrust and the virginity of the forest.

This language of violently contrary images subverts what we think of as 'ordinary', with its vocabulary and rhythm passed on to us by societal norms. To change language is to run the risk of chaos, but also to invite the kind of unreason that surrealism uses to transform speech and the world. 'If I am speaking only the language I have been taught, what will ever serve as a signal that we should listen to the voice of unreason, claiming that tomorrow will be *other*, that it is entirely and mysteriously separated from yesterday?', asked Breton. Everything is available to change and chance in this universe, made open to love, requiring a new and singular language appropriate to the lyric behaviour (*comportement lyrique*) that Breton saw as characteristic of surrealism. In this language and the vision it enables, the earth can be 'as blue as an orange' – not just for Paul Eluard but for us all.

The eroticising potential of words has never been more valued than within surrealism. As Breton puts it in his essay 'Words

Without Wrinkles' (*Les Mots sans rides*, 1922): 'let it be quite understood that when we say "word games", it is our surest reasons for living that are being put into play. Words, furthermore, have finished playing games. Words are making love.'

Translating surrealist love

All of which sets up an almost unbearably complex, if stimulating, challenge for the translator of surrealist texts. The weight placed on words means that each decision counts even more than in other poetries. Breton's great love poem of 1931, for example, originally written during the period of his turbulent relationship with Suzanne Muzard, but possibly for another woman, is significantly entitled 'Free union' (*L'Union libre*). The translation included here (p.24) is new, and had to be, for this self-renewing poem. Previous translations had given various interpretations of the repeated or anaphoric opening '*Ma femme ... Ma femme ...*' (the very repetition being part of an incantatory charm): 'My wife', or 'My woman', and so on. The statement of possession, which I would relate to the medieval and courtly love from which surrealism took so much, might then be thought of in terms of 'My lady', however outdated that terminology might be. It was tempting to use 'My beloved', since this would have left the love object free from any stifling claim of the macho sort ('My woman'), or the domesticating ('My wife'), retaining nevertheless both the love and its open expression, without the claim of ultimate possession. The final choice, 'My love', seemed to fulfill the same conditions more succinctly.

Many of the other poems here have been retranslated, often to make a fresh attempt at an unlimited and unlimiting vision. The

deliberate switches of rhythm give an exhilaration to the tenses of the
language, and the piling up of allusions in one word permit an explosion
into many new views of the object. So, in Breton's 'They tell me that
over there' (1934, p.32), the word *mal* (evil) is implicit in the original
French *la malle entr'ouverte* (the half-opened trunk) and explicit in
l'inexistence du mal (the nonexistence of evil). This suggests by linguistic
implication that the potential source of evil (*le mal*), connected with
the sound of maleness (*le mâle*), is restored to a state of innocence by
the image of the trunk, androgynous in its sound (*la malle*, as if it were
la mâle). For in this utopian universe, the rational and traditional limits
of gender – in their potentially destructive, single-gendered belligerence
– are transgressed, positively, by the shape-shifting muse of surrealist
love. Here, the melting-down of boundaries opens the poem and the
life of the lovers to the light of innocent vision.

Dream and the realm of the marvellous
The dream work of Freudian imagination also inspired
the dream work of surrealism, encouraging its faith in the unconscious
interconnection between the worlds of night and day, and in the
conscious awareness of how they excite each other. Nothing better
exemplifies this interconnection than Breton's poem 'I dream I see your
image' (1934, p.28), which interweaves all the elements of magic that
are possible and possibilising for the human mind within the world of
dream. The beloved, 'Caught in a bellows of spangles', skips her rope
until a wondrous vision, a green butterfly, appears on some 'unseen
stairs'. At the moment of the vision all her possibilities intensify ('I caress
all that you were/In all that you still will be'), and blossom into a magical

outpouring, symbolised by the 'crystal of the rose of winds' and the living fountain she becomes.

Typically, this poem also imports the visual into the textual, calling upon the highest possible potential of arousal. Precisely because the degree of control, both of self and of other, is so elevated in confrontation with the image, the mingling of sight and senses so potent, surrealist love poetry calls upon the look insistently, in full recognition of the conflagrations of opposites from which it can profit with the greatest urgency. The beloved represents the simultaneous vision characteristic of surrealist looking. Her multiple image is unlimited as imagination itself: 'I dream I see your image indefinitely imposed upon itself'. She is at the same moment seated before her mirror, combing her hair, and coming back from some voyage, having lingered 'last in the grotto/ Streaming with sparks'. Her every action is double, as her image is sparkling. Everything is miraculous in this highly visualised state, in which nothing is limited to a single place or moment: she is just falling asleep or just waking, where she was, or somewhere else. This indeterminacy of context and condition prevails in the boundless mental realm of the marvellous. Even the objects surrounding her are both single and multiplied a thousandfold: 'You are naked the elderberry still bounces/A thousand elderberries buzz above you'.

In this anti-rational universe, each participant is self-transforming, and transformative of the other. In Breton's *Arcanum 17* (1945), written after Jacqueline Lamba left him for the American painter David Hare, he invokes his love for his third wife, Elisa. The lover's muse is Melusina, a mermaid figure symbolising the feminine anti-rational attitude, the watery element dissolving all the weapons of war. Melusina the shape-shifter sings of the possibilities of surrealist love as non-restrictive, non-belligerent, endlessly transformative of both lover and beloved.

Perhaps no poem manifests the marvellous of surrealism more convincingly than Breton's 'They tell me that over there', from the collection 'The Air of Water' (1934, p.32). It describes a land of which others have told the poet, seen only as a mirage, in which contraries meet (black lava and snow), the hiss of the ocean's wave mingles with the sun's rays in all their alliterative splendour (*sous un second soleil de serins sauvages*), elements are turned upside down (the arms below the waist), and possibilities abound. When the question as to what land this might be is posed – a question that of course cannot be answered, just as desire must remain unsated – it is suggested that the beloved is the very source of its illumination, for it seems 'to take its light from [her] life', and its image is trembling 'at the tip of [her] lashes'.

The poem ends in a proof of redemption through a final image of contraries that perfectly exemplifies 'the one in the other' on which surrealist aesthetics is based: 'All the flowering appletree of the sea'. The appletree, so resonant with Adamic guilt, blooms once more in the openness of the blameless sea. Both natural elements are surrealised into a blossoming convergence, just as the human imagination is newly liberated into its ultimately dynamic, because continual, desire.

The immeasurable potency of surrealist writing, then, has a great deal to do with its unreasonable and thus all the more appealing optimism about love and the life it inhabits. The joyous intimacy of such a life surges into the present from the memory in poems like Joyce Mansour's 'Remember' of 1955 (p.88): the heart set ajolt, the hair ruffling, the couple laughing. Everything is intensified in this exalted state of sensory heightening, with the usual and the absurd given equal value in front of the intimate fact of being together – simple, ordinary and miraculous. Who, finally, is eating the poppies at the end of this poem? The rats running about the floor, or the lovers themselves? The answer is that the poem is constructed for both possibilities, and this is the province of surrealist poetry, as exemplified in René Char's 'The climate of the hunt or how poetry is made' (1934, p.43), which makes desire and pursuit synonymous with poetry, or Breton's 'On the road to San Romano' of 1948 (p.36), which ends: 'The embrace of poetry like that of the flesh/As long as it lasts/Shuts out any glimpse of the misery of the world'.

Several visual artists speak in this volume, and many generations are recognised, from countries outside of France: Remedios Varo, a Spanish artist who lived for most of her life in Mexico, the Spaniard Pablo Picasso and his lover the Franco-Yugloslav photographer and painter Dora Maar, Salvador Dalí, also from Spain, the Anglo-Egyptian Joyce Mansour, and the Mexican painter Frida Kahlo. The poems were chosen for their variety, just like the multifarious variety of amatory experiences in surrealism. Also included in these pages is a wide range of genres: from René Char's brief, two-line text called 'Love' (p.41), to his epic 'The nuptial countenance' (p.44); from the prose poem of Césaire, and the extract from Kahlo's journal, to the dream recipe of Varo. For the ways of love, and the surrealist expression of its always-remaining desire, are multicoloured, of many shapes, and of endless kinds. They will last, in the impossible possible of surrealism, both for a long time and forever.

The approach of love and a kiss

She stops at the stream's edge She sings
She runs She shouts up to the sky
Her dress opens on paradise
Her charm is infinite
She flutters hoop-wood over little waves
Slowly she passes her white hand over her pure forehead
Between her feet the weasels flee
In her hat sits heaven's blue

Poem written in the toilets with a knife on the wall

Put out the star	Listen from the
At the edge of the bed	Bottom of me
Milky white	My tempest
Horizontal	Rising towards you
Lovely bitterness	I have the name of you
Are you sleeping	Anger of you
Mouth of autumn	The immense jolt
Your breasts burned	Of loving
The night is nude	Here is the moment
Where there murmurs	Of fear
An unknown tongue	And the marvel
In my ear	To shout about
My orange oh	To shout to shout
My foreigner	To shout to shout
You my madness	Shout
And my woods	Shout
I am the wolf	I am I am
Devouring you	I am
The dogs who	DYING
Lick your feet	I am dying

Free union

My love whose hair is woodfire
Her thoughts heat lightning
Her waist an hourglass
My love an otter in the tiger's jaws
Her mouth a rosette bouquet of stars of the highest magnitude
Her teeth footprints of white mice on white earth
Her tongue smooth as amber and as glass
My love her tongue a sacred host stabbed through
Her tongue a doll whose eyes close and open
Her tongue a fantastic stone
Each eyelash traced by a child's hand
Her eyebrows the edge of a swallow's nest
My love her temples slates on a greenhouse roof
And their misted panes
My love whose shoulders are champagne
And the dolphin heads of a fountain under ice
My love her wrists thin as matchsticks
Whose fingers are chance and the ace of hearts
Whose fingers are mowed hay
My love with marble and beechnut beneath her arms
Of Midsummer night
Of privet and the nests of angel fish
Whose arms are sea foam and river locks
And the mingling of wheat and mill
My love whose legs are fireworks
Moving like clockwork and despair
My love her calves of elder tree marrow

My love whose feet are initial letters
Are key rings and sparrows drinking
My love her neck pearled with barley
My love her throat of a golden valley
Rendez-vous in the torrent's very bed
Her breasts of night
My love her breasts molehills beneath the sea
Crucibles of rubies
Spectre of the dew-sparkled rose
My love whose belly unfurls the fan of every day
Its giant claws
Whose back is a bird's vertical flight
Whose back is quicksilver
Whose back is light
The nape of her neck is crushed stone and damp chalk
And the fall of a glass where we just drank
My love whose hips are wherries
Whose hips are chandeliers and feathers
And the stems of white peacock plumes
Imperceptible in their sway
My love whose buttocks are of sandstone
Of swan's back and amianthus
And of springtime
My love whose sex is gladiolus
Is placer and platypus
Algae and sweets of yore
Is mirror

André Breton

My love her eyes full of tears
Of violet panoply and magnetic needle
My love of savannah eyes
My love her eyes of water to drink in prison
My love her eyes of wood always to be chopped
Eyes of water level earth and air and fire

André Breton

I dream I see your image

I dream I see your image indefinitely imposed upon itself
You are seated on the high coral stool
Before your mirror still in its first quarter
Two fingers on the water wing of your comb
And at the same time
You are returning from a trip lingering last in the grotto
Streaming with sparks
You do not know me
You are lying on the bed you wake where you fall asleep
You wake where you fell asleep or elsewhere
You are naked the elderberry still bounces
A thousand elderberries buzz above you
So light that at every moment
Unbeknownst to you
Your breath your blood saved from the air's mad juggling
You cross the street the cars that rush at you turn to a shadow
And the same
Child
Caught in a bellows of spangles
You are skipping rope
Until atop the unseen stairs appears
The sole green butterfly that haunts the Asian peaks
I caress all that you were
In all that you still will be
I hear your countless arms
Whistling tunefully
Snake unique in all the trees

André Breton

In your arms turns the crystal of the rose of winds
My living fountain of Shiva

Always for the first time

Always for the first time
I scarcely know you when I see you
You return sometime in the night
To a house at an angle to my window
A wholly imaginary house
From one second to the next
There in the complete darkness
I wait for the strange rift to recur
The unique rift
In the façade and in my heart
The nearer I come to you
In reality
The louder the key sings in the door of the unknown room
Where you appear alone before me
First you merge with the brightness
The fleeting angle of a curtain
A jasmine field I gazed on at dawn on a road near Grasse
The jasmine-pickers bending over on a slant
Behind them the dark profile of plants stripped bare
Before them the dazzling light
The curtain invisibly raised
In a frenzy all the flowers swarm back
You facing this long hour never dim enough until sleep
You as if you could be
The same except I may never meet you
You pretend not to know I'm watching you
Marvellously I'm no longer sure you know it

Your idleness fills my eyes with tears
Meanings surround each of your gestures
Like a honeydew hunt
There are rocking-chairs on a bridge there are branches
That might scratch you in the forest
In a window on the rue Notre-Dame-de-Lorette
Two lovely crossed legs are caught in long stockings
Flaring out in the centre of a great white clover
There is a silk ladder unrolled across the ivy
There is
That leaning over the precipice
Of the hopeless fusion of your presence and absence
I have found the secret
Of loving you
Always for the first time

André Breton

They tell me that over there

> They tell me that over there the beaches are black
> From the lava running to the sea
> Stretched out at the foot of a great peak smoking with snow
> Under a second sun of wild canaries
> So what is this far-off land
> Seeming to take its light from your life
> It trembles very real at the tip of your lashes
> Sweet to your carnation like an intangible linen
> Freshly pulled from the half-open trunk of the ages
> Behind you
> Casting its last sombre fires between your legs
> The earth of the lost paradise
> Glass of shadows mirror of love
> And lower towards your arms opening
> On the proof by springtime
> OF AFTERWARDS
> Of evil's not existing
> All the flowering appletree of the sea

As they move

As they move your limbs unfold about you sheets of green
And the outer world
Speckled
No longer plays
Meadows have faded the days
Bell towers rejoin
And the social puzzle
Has given up its last setting
This morning yet again these sheets rose up
Set sail with you from a prismatic bed
In the willow castle blurry with lama eyes
Towards which head downwards
I set off once
Sheets almond of my life
When you walk the Venus copper
Unnerves the slick edgeless leaf
Your large liquid wing
Flutters in the glazier's song

André Breton

In the lovely twilight

In the lovely twilight of 1934
The air was a splendid red mullet rose
And the forest I was about to enter
Began by a tree with cigarette paper leaves
Because I was awaiting you
And when you walk with me
No matter where
The blue wheel diffuse and broken starts off from
Your enamel mouth to rise
And turn pale in the rut
All the marvels rushed to meet me
A squirrel had come to touch its white stomach to my heart
I don't know how he held there
But the earth was full of reflections deeper than the water's
As if the metal had finally shaken off its shell
And you lying on the frightening sea of stones
You were turning
Naked
In a great sun of fireworks
I saw you slowly descend from the radiolaria
Even in the sea urchin shells I was there
Forgive me I was there no longer
I had raised my head for the living sheath of white velvet
Had left me
And I was sad
The sky between the leaves shone haggard and harsh
Like a dragonfly

I was going to close my eyes
When the two wood panels pulled apart fell
Without noise
Like the two central leaves of a great lily of the valley
A flower able to contain the whole night
I was where you see me
In the perfume sounded in full peal
Before they came back to life
I had time to place my lips
On your thighs of glass

André Breton

On the road to San Romano

Poetry is made in a bed like love
Its rumpled sheets are the dawn of things
Poetry is made in the woods

It has the space it needs
Not this one but the other whose form is lent it by
        The eye of the kite
        The dew on a horsetail
        The memory of a bottle frosted over on a silver tray
        A tall rod of tourmaline on the sea
        And the road of the mental adventure
        That climbs abruptly
        One stop and bushes cover it instantly

That isn't to be shouted on the rooftops
It's improper to leave the door open
Or to summon witnesses

        The shoals of fish the hedges of titmice
        The rails at the entrance of a great station
        The reflections of both riverbanks
        The crevices in the bread
        The bubbles of the stream
        The days of the calendar
        The St John's wort

The acts of love and poetry
Are incompatible
With reading the newspaper aloud

The meaning of the sunbeam
The blue light between the hatchet blows
The bat's thread shaped like a heart or a hoopnet
The beavers' tails beating in time
The diligence of the flash
The casting of candy from the old stairs
The avalanche

The room of marvels
No dear sirs it isn't the eighth Chamber
Nor the vapours of the roomful some Sunday evening

The figures danced transparent above the pools
The outline on the wall of a woman's body at
daggerthrow
The bright spirals of smoke
The curls of your hair
The curve of the Philippine sponge
The swaying of the coral snake
The ivy entrance in the ruins
It has all the time ahead

The embrace of poetry like that of the flesh
As long as it lasts
Shuts out any glimpse of the misery of the world

I love

I love *sliding* I love *upsetting everything*
I love *coming in* I love *sighing*
I love *taming the furtive manes of hair*
I love *hot* I love *tenuous*
I love *supple* I love *infernal*
I love *sugared but elastic the curtain of* springs *turning to glass*
I love *pearl* I love *skin*
I love *tempest* I love *pupil*
I love *benevolent seal* long-distance *swimmer*
I love *oval* I love *struggling*
I love *shining* I love *breaking*
I love *the smoking spark* silk *vanilla mouth to mouth*
I love *blue* I love *known* – knowing
I love *lazy* I love *spherical*
I love *liquid* beating drum *sun if it wavers*
I love *to the left* I love *in the fire*
I love *because* I love *at the edges*
I love *forever many times* Just one
I love *freely* I love *especially*
I love *separately* I love *scandalously*
I love *similarly obscurely uniquely*

HOPINGLY

I love   I shall love

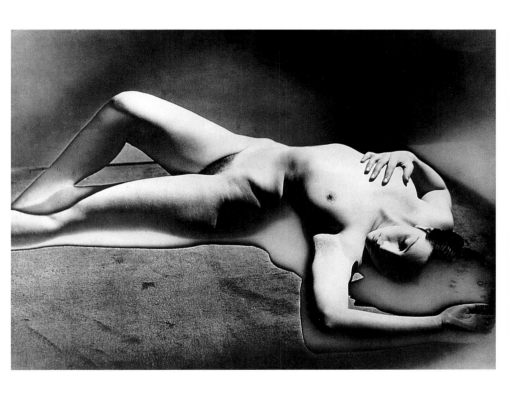

The automatic crystal

hello hello night again don't worry about it this is
your cave man speaking grasshoppers whose life
is as dizzy as their death green lagoon water even
drowned that will never be my colour thinking of
you I have to pawn all my words a whole stream of
bathing beauties in their sleds as the day goes by
gold as the bread and the wine of your breasts hello
hello I'd like to be on the earth's bright underside
the tip of your breasts looks and tastes like that hello
hello night again the rain has gravedigger fingers
the rain tripping over itself on the roofs the rain ate
the sun with chopsticks hello hello in growth of a
crystal it's you... it's you oh absence in the wind and
serpentine bather at dawn you'll set the river of
your eyes on the enamel of the islands slipping by
and in my head you're the dazzling maguey tree
from the tide of eagles under the banyan

Love

To be
The first to come.

The climate of the hunt or how poetry is made

My pure sobbing followed by its poison: the brain of my love wooed by the bottle shards.

Ah! in the house of eclipses, let the dominant one, withdrawing, bring darkness. At last we'll delay the advance of storms in the rapids of dusk.

In love, there's still immobility, this gigantic sex.

Late at night we went out to gather the fruits needed for my death dreams: those violet figs.

The archaic dead horses in the shape of a bathtub pass by and fade out. Only the manure speaks to reassure us.

When I leave for a long time in a faceless world, the serenity of steam by the bedside of the great orange tree.

In my extreme ecstasy a young girl appears with an amanita waist, cuts the throat of a cock, then falls into a deep sleep, while a little way from her bed there runs a stream and its dangers. Sending sent away.

Violence of love forbidden
Instant asphyxiation of a diamond
Paralysis wandering sweetness.

The nuptial countenance

Now let my escort disappear, standing in the distance;
numbers have just lost their sweetness.
I give you leave, my allies, my violent ones, my indices.
Everything summons you away, fawning sorrow.
I am in love.

Water is heavy at a day's flow from the spring.
The crimson foliage crosses its slow branches at your forehead, dimension reassured.
And I, like you,
with the straw in flower at the edge of the sky crying your name,
I cut down the traces,
stricken, strong in clarity.

Ring of vapour, many made supple, dividers of fear, touch my renewal.
Walls of my enduring, I renounce the succour of my venial breadth;
I timber the device of the dwelling, I thwart the first fruits of survivals.
Afire with itinerant solitude,
I evoke the swimming on the shade of her Presence.

The desert body hostile to an alloyage, had returned yesterday, speaking darkly.
Decline, do not halt your movement, drop your bludgeon of seizures, acrid sleep.
Indentation diminishes the bones of your exile, of your sparring;
you freshen constraint self-devouring;
gust of the night, halt this grim cartage
of glazed voices, stone-pelted departures.

Soon subtracted from the flux of contriving lesions
(the eagle's pickaxe flings high the flaring blood)
across a present destiny I have led my exemptions

toward an azure multivalved, granite dissidence.

O vaulted effusion upon the crown of her belly,
murmurings of dark dowry!
O the exhausted motion of her diction!
Nativity, guide the unyielding, may they find their foundations,
the almond believable in the fresh day to come.
Evening has closed its corsair's gash where the rockets soared aimlessly amid
    a dogged fear.
Past now the micas of mourning on your face.

Unquenchable pane: my breath was already grazing the friendship of your wound,
arming your hidden royalty.
And from the lips of the fog descended our joy with its threshold of dune, its
    roof of steel.
Awareness increased the quivering array of your permanence;
faithful simplicity spread everywhere.

Tone of morning's adage, slack season of the early star,
I rush to the term of my arch, interred coliseum.
Long enough embraced the nubile hair of grain:
O stubborn one, carder, our reaches force its submission.
Long enough condemned the haven of nuptial semblances:
I touch the depths of a compact return.

Streams, neuma of the craggy dead,
you who follow the arid sky,
mingle your going with his storms, who could heal desertion,
striking against your saving studies.

René Char

At the roof's centre bread suffocates carrying heart and light.
Take, oh my Thought, the flower of my penetrable hand,
Feel the dark planting waken.
I shall not see your sides, those swarms of hunger, dry up, fill with brambles;
I shall not see the mantis replace you in your greenhouse;
I shall not see the minstrels approach, disquieting the reborn day;
I shall not see our freedom's lineage servile in self-sufficiency.

Chimeras, we have climbed upland.
Flint quivered beneath vine-shoots of space;
The word, tired of battering, drank at the angelic wharf.
No savage survival:
The horizon of roads to the abounding dew,
Intimate unfolding of the irreparable.

This is the sand dead, this the body saved:
Woman breathes, Man stands upright.

Salvador Dalí

Binding cradled – cradle bound

Perduring binding
at the same time unjustly declining
a cup
some Portuguese cup
now manufactured
in a china factory
for a cup
its shape resembles
a sweet municipal Arab antinomy
set or seen thereabouts
like the gaze of my lovely Gala
the gaze of my lovely Gala
smell of wine dregs
like the epithelial tissue of my lovely Gala
her funny lamplighting epithelial tissue

yes I shall say it a thousand times over

Perduring binding
at the same time unjustly declining
a cup
some Portuguese cup
now manufactured
in a china factory
for a cup
its shape resembles
a sweet municipal Arab antinomy
set or seen thereabouts

like the gaze of my lovely Gala
the gaze of my lovely Gala
smell of wine dregs
like the epithelial tissue of my lovely Gala
her funny lamplighting epithelial tissue

yes I shall say it a thousand times over

Through the half-opened window

on my disdain of the world
a breeze was rising
perfumed with stephanotis
while you drew towards YOURSELF
the whole curtain

Such
do I see you
shall I always see you
drawing towards yourself
the whole curtain of the poem
where
God you are lovely
but so long getting naked

I have so often dreamed of you

I have so often dreamed of you that you become unreal.
Is it still time enough to reach that living body and to kiss
on that mouth the birth of the voice so dear to me?
I have so often dreamed of you that my arms used as they are
to meet on my breast in embracing your shadow would
perhaps not fit the contour of your body.
And, before the real appearance of what has haunted and ruled
me for days and years, I might become only a shadow.
Oh the weighing of sentiment.
I have so often dreamed of you that there is probably no time
now to waken. I sleep standing, my body exposed to all the
appearances of life and love and you, who alone still
matter to me, I could less easily touch your forehead and
your lips than the first lips and the first forehead I
might meet by chance.
I have so often dreamed of you, walked, spoken, slept with your
phantom that perhaps I can be nothing any longer than a
phantom among phantoms and a hundred times more
shadow than the shadow which walks and will walk
joyously over the sundial of your life.

No, love is not dead

No, love is not dead in this heart and these eyes and this mouth which
     announced the beginning of its burial.
Listen, I have had enough of the picturesque and the colourful and
     the charming.
I love love, its tenderness and cruelty.
My love has but one name, but one form.
All passes. Mouths press against this mouth.
My love has but one name, but one form.
And if some day you remember
O form and name of my love,
One day on the ocean between America and Europe,
At the hour when the last sunbeam reverberates on the undulating surface
     of waves, or else a stormy night beneath a tree in the countryside or in
     a speeding car,
A spring morning on the boulevard Malesherbes,
A rainy day,
At dawn before sleeping,
Tell yourself, I command your familiar spirit, that I alone loved you more
     and that it is sad you should not have known it.
Tell yourself one must not regret things: Ronsard before me and
     Baudelaire have sung the regrets of ladies old or dead who despised
     the purest love.
When you are dead
You will be beautiful and always desirable
I will already be dead, enclosed forever complete within your immortal
     body, in your astonishing image present forever among the constant
     marvels of life and of eternity, but if I live

Your voice and its tone, your look and its radiance,
Your fragrance, the scent of your hair and many other things
    besides will still live in me,
Who am neither Ronsard nor Baudelaire,
I who am Robert Desnos and who for having known and loved you,
Am easily their equal.
I who am Robert Desnos, to love you
Wanting nothing else to be remembered by on the
    despicable earth.

Robert Desnos

If you knew

Far from me and like the stars, the sea, and all the props of poetic legend,
Far from me and present all the same without your knowing,
Far from me and still more silent since I imagine you endlessly,
Far from me, my beautiful mirage and my eternal dream, you cannot know.
If you knew.
Far from me and perhaps still farther from being unaware of me and
    still unaware.
Far from me because you doubtless do not love me or, not so different,
    I doubt your love.
Far from me because you cleverly ignore my passionate desires.
Far from me for you are cruel.
If you knew.
Far from me, oh joyous as the flower dancing in the river on its watery
    stem, oh sad as seven in the evening in the mushroom fields.
Far from me still silent as in my presence and still joyous as the stork-
    shaped hour falling from on high.
Far from me at the moment when the alembics sing, when the silent
    and noisy sea curls up on the white pillows.
If you knew.
Far from me, oh my present present torment, far from me with the
    splendid sound of oyster shells crunched under the nightwalker's
    step, at dawn, when he passes by the door of restaurants.
If you knew.
Far from me, willed and material mirage.
Far from me an island turns aside at the passing of ships.
Far from me a calm herd of cattle mistakes the patch, stops stubbornly
    at the brink of a steep precipice, far from me, oh cruel one.

Far from me, a shooting star falls in the night bottle of the poet. He corks it
instantly to watch the star enclosed within the glass, the constellations
come to life against the sides, far from me, you are far from me.
If you knew.
Far from me a house is built just now.
A white-clothed worker atop the structure sings a sad brief song and
suddenly, in the hod of mortar there appears the future of the house:
lovers' kisses and double suicides and nakedness in the rooms of
lovely unknown girls and their midnight dreams, and the voluptuous
secrets surprised by the parquet floors.
Far from me,
If you knew.
If you knew how I love you and though you do not love me, how I am
happy, how I am strong and proud, with your image in my mind, to
leave the universe.
How I am happy enough to perish from it.
If you knew how the world submits to me.
And you, oh beautiful unsubmissive one, how you are my prisoner.
Oh far-from-me to whom I submit.
If you knew.

Sleep spaces

In the night there are naturally the seven marvels of the world and
    greatness and the tragic and enchantment.
Confusedly, forests mingle with legendary creatures hidden in the
    thickets.
You are there.
In the night there is the nightwalker's step and the murderer's and the
    policeman's and the streetlight and the ragman's lantern.
You are there.
In the night pass trains and ships and the mirage of countries where it
    is daylight. The last breaths of twilight and the first shivers of dawn.
You are there.
A tune on the piano, an exclamation.
A door slams,
A clock.
And not just beings and things and material noises.
But still myself chasing myself or going on beyond.
You are there, immolated one, you for whom I wait.
Sometimes strange figures are born at the instant of sleep and
    disappear.
When I close my eyes, phosphorescent blooms appear and fade and
    are reborn like carnal fireworks.
Unknown countries I traverse with creatures for company.
You are there most probably, oh beautiful discreet spy.
And the palpable soul of the reaches.
And the perfumes of the sky and the stars and the cock's crow from
    two thousand years ago and the peacock's scream in the parks
    aflame and kisses.

Handshakes sinister in a sickly light and axles screeching on
hypnotic roads.
You are most probably there, whom I do not know, whom on the
contrary I know.
But who, present in my dreams, insist on being sensed there without
appearing.
You who remain out of reach in reality and in dream.
You who belong to me by my will to possess you in illusion but whose face
approaches mine only if my eyes are closed to dream as well as to
reality.
You in spite of an easy rhetoric where waves die on the beaches, where the
crow flies in ruined factories, where wood rots cracking under a
leaden sun.
You who are at the depths of my dreams, full of metamorphoses and
leaving me your glove when I kiss your hand.
In the night there are stars and the obscure motion of the sea, rivers,
forests, towns, grass, the lungs of millions and millions of beings.
In the night there are the marvels of the world.
In the night there are no guardian angels but there is sleep.
In the night you are there.
In the day as well.

Oh pangs of love!

Oh pangs of love!
How necessary you are to me and how precious.
My eyes closing on imaginary tears, my hands stretching
    out ceaselessly toward nothingness.
I dreamed last night of crazed landscapes and of adventures
    as dangerous from the perspective of death as from the
    perspective of life which are both also the perspective of love.
At my waking you were present, oh pangs of love, oh desert
    muses, oh exigent muses.
My laugh and my joy crystallise about you. Your
make-up, your powder, your rouge, your snakeskin bag, your
silk stockings... and also that little fold between the ear
and the nape of your neck, near its base, your
silk stockings and your delicate blouse and your fur coat, your
round belly is my laughter and your feet my joys and
all your jewels.
Really, how good-looking and well dressed you are.
Oh pangs of love, exigent angels, here I am imagining you
    in the very likeness of my love, confusing you with her...
Oh pangs of love, you whom I create and clothe, you
    are confused with my love of whom I know only her clothes
    and also her eyes, voice, face, hands, hair, teeth, eyes...

Never anyone but you

Never anyone but you in spite of stars and solitudes
In spite of mutilated trees at nightfall
Never anyone but you will take a path which is mine also
The farther you go away the greater your shadow grows
Never anyone but you will salute the sea at dawn when tired of wandering
    having left the dark-shadowed forests and thistle bushes I shall walk
    toward the foam
Never anyone but you will place her hand on my forehead and my eyes
Never anyone but you and I deny falsehood and infidelity
This anchored boat you may cut its rope
Never anyone but you
The eagle prisoner in a cage pecks slowly at the copper bars turned green
What an escape!
It's Sunday marked by the song of nightingales in the woods of a tender
    green the tedium felt by little girls before a cage where a canary flies
    about while in the solitary street the sun slowly moves its narrow line
    across the heated sidewalk
We shall pass other lines
Never never anyone but you
And I alone like the faded ivy of suburban gardens alone like glass
And you never anyone but you.

Robert Desnos

The voice of Robert Desnos

So like the flower and the breeze
like the water's flowing with its passing shadows
like the smile glimpsed that famous midnight
so like everything like joy and sadness
it's past midnight its naked torso rising above belfries and poplars
I summon to me all those lost in the countryside
old corpses young felled oaks
the threads of cloth rotting on the ground and the linen drying
        near the farms
I summon to me tornadoes and hurricanes
tempests typhoons cyclones
tidal waves
earthquakes
I summon to me volcano smoke and that of cigarettes
smoke rings from luxury cigars
I summon to me loves and lovers
I summon to me the living and the dead
I summon to me gravediggers I summon murderers
I summon executioners I summon pilots builders and architects
murderers
I summon flesh
I summon the one I love
I summon the one I love
I summon the one I love
triumphant midnight unfolds its satin wings and alights on my bed
belfries and poplars bend to my desire
the former fall in ruin the latter fade

those lost in the countryside find their way in finding me
the old cadavers resuscitate at my voice
the young felled oaks turn green
the shreds of cloth rotting in the ground and on the ground
clack at my voice like the banner of rebellion
the linen drying around the farms dresses adorable women
    whom I do not adore
who come to me obey my voice and adore me
tornadoes twist in my mouth
hurricanes redden my lips even more
tempests growl at my feet
typhoons rumple my hair even more
I receive the drunken kisses of cyclones
tidal waves rush forward to die at my feet
earthquakes destroy only at my command
volcano smoke clothes me in its vapours
and cigarette smoke perfumes me
and smoke rings from cigars crown me
loves and love so long pursued take refuge in me
lovers listen to my voice
the living and the dead submit to me the former greeting me
    coldly the latter in friendship
gravediggers leave graves half dug declaring that I alone can
    order their nightly labour
murderers salute me
executioners invoke the revolution
invoke my voice

invoke my name
pilots steer according to my eyes
builders grow dizzy listening to me
architects leave for the desert
murderers bless me
flesh quivers at my call
the one I love does not listen to me
the one I love does not hear me
the one I love does not answer me

Robert Desnos

Obsession

I bring you a bit of seaweed which was tangled with the sea foam and
    this comb
But your hair is more neatly fixed than the clouds tossed by winds with
    celestial crimson glowing in them and are such that with quiverings
    of life and sobs twisting sometimes between my hands they die with the
    waves and the reefs of the strand so abundantly that we shall not soon
    again despair of perfumes and their flight at evening when this comb
    marks motionless the stars buried in their rapid and silky flow traversed
    by my hands seeking still at their root the humid caress of a sea more
    dangerous than the one where this seaweed was gathered with the froth
    scattered by a tempest
A star dying is like your lips
They turn blue as the wine spilled on the tablecloth
An instant passes with a mine's profundity
With a muffled complaint the anthracite falls in flakes on the town
How cold it is in the impasse where I knew you
A forgotten number on a house in ruins
Number 4 I think
Before too long I'll find you again near these China asters
The mines make a muffled snoring
The roofs are strewn with anthracite
This comb in your hair like the end of the world
The smoke the old bird and the jay
There the roses and the emeralds are finished
The precious stones and the flowers
The earth crumbles and stars screeching like an iron across mother-of-pearl
But your neatly fixed hair has the shape of a hand.

Your mouth with golden lips

Your mouth with golden lips does not laugh in me
And your halo words make such perfect sense
That in my nights of years, of youth and death
I hear your voice vibrant through all the world's sounds.

In this dawn of silk where cold lies still
Lust endangered misses sleep,
In the sun's hands all the bodies waking
Shiver at the thought of finding their heart again.

Remembering green woods, I sink into fog,
Closing my eyes on myself, I am all yours,
My whole life listens to you and I cannot undo
The terrible freedoms your love creates for me.

Paul Eluard

The shape of your eyes

The shape of your eyes goes round my heart,
A round of dance and sweetness.
Halo of time, cradle nightly and sure
No longer do I know what I've lived,
Your eyes have not always seen me.

Leaves of day and moss of dew,
Reeds of wind and scented smiles,
Wings lighting up the world,
Boats laden with sky and sea,
Hunters of sound and sources of colour,

Scents the echoes of a covey of dawns
Recumbent on the straw of stars,
As the day depends on innocence
The world relies on your pure sight
All my blood courses in its glance.

I love you

I love you for all the women I have not known
I love you for all the times I have not lived
For the smell of the vast sea and of warm bread
For the melting snow for the first flowers
For the pure beasts unafraid of man
I love you for loving
I love you for all the women I do not love

Who reflects me except you I see myself so seldom
Without you I see nothing but a desert waste
Between the present and the past
All these deaths I've traversed on straw
I have not pierced my mirror's wall
I had to learn life word by word
As you forget

I love you for your wisdom that is not mine
For health
I love you against all illusion
For this immortal heart I do not hold
You think you are doubt and you are but reason
You are the great sun arousing me
When I am sure of myself.

Paul Eluard

The earth is blue like an orange

> The earth is blue like an orange
> Never an error words do not lie
> They no longer supply what to sing with
> It's up to kisses to get along
> Mad ones and lovers
> She her wedding mouth
> All secrets all smiles
> And what indulgent clothing
> She looks quite naked.
>
> The wasps are flowering green
> Dawn is placing round its neck
> A necklace of windows
> Wings cover the leaves
> You have all the solar joys
> All sunshine on the earth
> On the paths of your loveliness.

I've told you

I've told you for the clouds
Told you for the ocean's tree
For each wave for birds in the leaves
For the small stones of sound
For the familiar hands
For the eye changing to face or landscape
And sleep restores colour to the sky
For all the night drunk deep
For the grillwork of the roads
For the window opened for a forehead laid bare
I've told you for your thoughts your words
Every caress every confidence survives.

As you rise

As you rise waters unfold
As you lie down the waters spread

You are the water led from its depths
You are the earth taking root
On which all things are built

You shape globes of silence in the desert of sounds
You sing nightly hymns on the ropes of rainbow
You are everywhere you annul all roads

You sacrifice time
To the eternal youth of the exact flame
Veiling nature reproducing it

Woman you give birth to a body always the same
Your own

You are resemblance.

Paul Eluard

The lover

She is standing on my eyelids
And her hair is in my hair,
She has the shape of my hands,
The colour of my eyes,
She is absorbed in my shadow,
Like a stone upon the sky.

She keeps her eyes open
And doesn't let me sleep.
Her dreams in broad daylight
Make the suns evaporate,
Make me laugh, weep and laugh,
And speak, without a thing to say.

About one, two, everyone

I am observer actor and author
I am the woman her husband and their child
And the first love and the last one
The furtive passer-by and the love abashed

And again the woman her bed and gown
And her arms shared and the man's work
And his love shooting forth and her female waves
Simple and double my flesh is never in exile

For where body lives I begin consciousness and form
And even when it is undone in death
I lie down in its hollow I espouse its torment
Its infamy honours my heart and my life.

Since it must be

In the full bed your body turns simple
Liquid sex universe of liquid
Linking the waters so many bodies
Whole entire from nape to ankle
Skinless mound maternal mound in travail
Servile mound agleam with blood
Between breasts thighs and buttocks
Controlling shade extracting warmth
Lip stretched to the bed's horizon
Lacking a sponge to absorb the night
Lacking all sleep to look like death.

Our life

Our life you made, it is buried
Dawn of a town a fine May morning
On which the earth has closed its fist
Dawn in me seventeen years always brighter
And death enters in me like a mill

Our life you said, so happy to live
And to give life to what we loved
But death has smashed time's scales
Death coming death going death lived
Death visible eats and drinks at my cost

Death visible Nusch invisible harsher
Than hunger and thirst to my worn-out body
Mask of snow on and under the earth
Spring of tears in the night mask of a blind man
My past dissolves I give way to silence

You came down from the mountains

You came down from the mountains
red steps of the great temples
you travelled the world
with the haughty silhouette
of a Prometheus
chained standing
you went toward the island
hemmed with Brussels lace
and with clashing ermines
of flowing luxury.
The girl of Irish velvet
and of elsewhere
lying on skins of lions
tigers and boredom
killed by her father
listened on the woods of the islands
for the step of the one
who would make her life resonate
and would rig up the full sails
of the adventurers in gold and steel.
Once in a while the sea-green wind
bent the rushes
in the dark places.

Now he comes

Now he comes, my hand, my red vision. larger. more
yours. martyr of glass. The great unreason. Columns and
valleys. the fingers of the wind. bleeding children. the
micron mica. I do not know what my joking dream thinks.
The ink, the spot. the form. the colour. I am a bird. I am
everything, without more confusion. All the bells, the
rules. The lands. the great grove, the greatest tenderness.
the immense tide. garbage. bathtub. letters of cardboard.
dice, fingers duets weak hope of making construction. the
cloths. the kings. so stupid. my nails. the thread and the
hair. the playful nerve I'm going now with myself. An
absent minute. You've been stolen from me and I'm
leaving crying. He is a waverer.

Twelfth ring (extract)

My love, I've dared to speak just of me in order to cry with you that tragedy abounds through the lack of means, that the comic strips of violence are only the little sounding-balloons of a fool's bother.

You are always free to slam the portals of your eyelids for other departures. I won't hold you back with any proselytising chewing gum, I won't ever wound you with the flamethrower of an initiate refusing to breathe. All doors are open like my legs at your approach, swinging open like my dress in its frenzy by the sea.

I have followed you, like others, in the night along the river, because I had the impression that evening that some – and I'm not saying we – could give life to all the city's desires, still trembling disarmingly in spite of everything under the asphalt.

I'm not afraid, I am calmly going down the steps losing their precision under the eyes of day, but certain beforehand that the advancing of each circle of water around my leg upsets the thermic system of an individuality easily admitted. (Don't laugh, you on the shore; once in the current, you'll see that the municipal buoys don't help at all.)

My love, I'm not following you, perhaps I am sweeping you along, myself or some women whose faces you find at the meeting of rivers. I don't hope that their reflection speaks to you only of me. I am not claiming to go to your ultimate depths when every notion of limit takes its basis on the scabs of a shamefully Christian nonsense; it's only the incongruous relation of multiple presences around you that will violate you as you wish. From you, from the others, from myself, I want the fire it is always possible to spark forth from between the stones of time; but the fire is no one's, the fire devours the relations of cause to effect, will always find itself in the gazes that we don't yet know.

Oh you dissatisfied of every kind, don't warm up to the idea of a new mode of violence that you could wear, without danger, in town as in the country, and throw away, after using it, at the bottom of the coffin-beds of some up-to-date individualism, like a Great Inquisitor of desire set free.

Sulphur smile

Muses, you preside over the imaginary rape of the lovely
    passers-by who smite our heart.
Two girls were walking with noble stride, naked as seaweed
    under their skirt. I moved forward to seize them. They
    refused my caresses and began to insult me. Then I threw
    them down upon the ground. My heel smashed into their
    faces. They became chimeras. Their breasts burst open and
    flew off... Finally they reassured me.
Oh girls! Oh desire! Oh crime!
Muses, fierce advisers, tell me FOR WHOM are these women.
You too, are a woman, oh solitude; you love me, I know, but
    really your jealousy is pitiless.

Dora Maar

I rested in the arms of my arms

     I rested in the arms of my arms
     I no longer slept
     It was night in the summer, winter in the day
     An eternal shivering of thoughts
     Fear love Fear love
     Close the window open the window
     You'll see you'll see
     The hummingbird motionless as a star

Your breath in my mouth

Your breath in my mouth
The pointed nails of your dry hands
Will never loose my crimson throat
Crimson from shame pain pleasure.
Your violet lips will suck my blood
And my waxen flesh still tempt you
As long as my eyes stay closed.

Joyce Mansour

You love to lie in our unmade bed

You love to lie in our unmade bed.
Our old sweats do not disgust you.
Our sheets soiled by forgotten dreams
Our cries that sound in the dark room
All this exalts your starved body.
Your ugly face lights up at last
For our past desires are your tomorrow's dreams.

I want to show myself naked

I want to show myself naked to your singing eyes.
Want you to see me shout with pleasure.
Want my limbs bent under such a weight
To urge you to disgraceful acts.
Want the smooth hair of my offered head
To cling to your nails curved with fury.
Want you to stand upright blind believing
Looking from high up at my plucked body.

Joyce Mansour

The storm sketches a silver margin

The storm sketches a silver margin
In the sky
And bursts in a great sticky spasm
On the ground.
The floating foam
Cast up by the receding sea
Comes to cool our tired faces
And our bodies hiding
In the tepid dark of our sleeping desires
Stand up straight.
Our nap the lice have plagued
Ends
And the brief lapping of the waves
On the beach where the azure dances
Has fallen quiet, my love,
And it's raining.

Remember

Remember
The jolting flight of my heart
Your excitement
The way my hair ruffles
When I laugh with you
The wind stuffed with smells
Coming before my body aflame
The rubbery grey thickness of the winter evenings
When we heard the rats jingling around
Eating poppies
You and me.

I want to sleep with you

I want to sleep with you side by side
Our hair intertwined
Our sexes joined
With your mouth for a pillow.
I want to sleep with you back to back
With no breath to part us
No words to distract us
No eyes to lie to us
With no clothes on.
To sleep with you breast to breast
Tense and sweating
Shining with a thousand quivers
Consumed by ecstatic mad inertia
Stretched out on your shadow
Hammered by your tongue
To die in a rabbit's rotting teeth
Happy.

Even long after my death

Even long after my death
Long after your death
I want to torture you.
I want the thought of me
to coil around your body like a serpent of fire
without burning you.

I want to see you lost, asphyxiated, wander
in the murky haze
woven by my desires.

For you, I want long sleepless nights
filled by the roaring tom-tom of storms
Far away, invisible, unknown.
Then, I want the nostalgia of my presence
to paralyse you.

Turtledove on the ground

Turtledove on the ground
seeking coral for its lamp
Breasts in freedom flying singing
contrary to the magpie filled with song
invisible in the damp tree
Female voices at the forest's edge
beneath the fan-shaped paw
sowing a field of clouds
above the barley terrace

The magnetic forest weaves away
forest of fruits with sexes mingled
slow loves mimicked in the vines
this leaf looks at me
with empty orbs
deep in the flying garden

Alice Paalen

A woman who was beautiful

A woman who was beautiful
one day
removed her face
her head became smooth
blind and deaf
safe from the snares of mirrors
and from looks of love

amid the reeds of the sun
her head hatched by a sparrowhawk
could not be found

secrets much more beautiful
for not having been said
words not written
steps erased
nameless ashes flown away
without marble plaque
desecrating memory

so many wings to break
before nightfall.

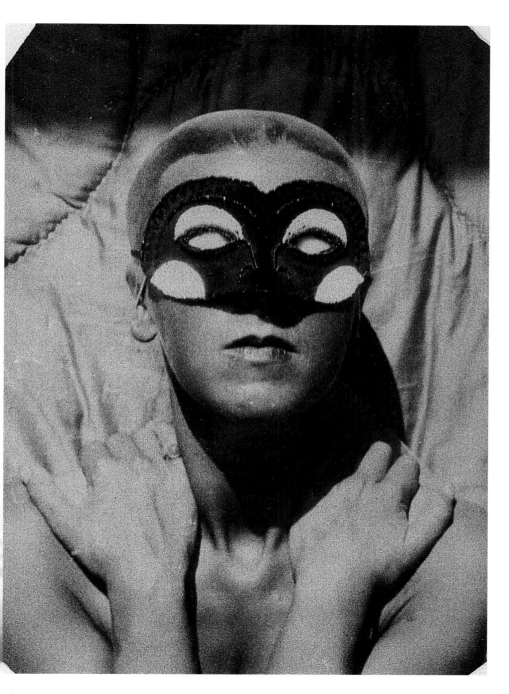

Clear night (extract)

The city unfolds
its face is the face of my love
its legs are the legs of a woman
Towers plazas columns bridges streets
river belt of drowned landscapes
City or Woman Presence
fan that reveals or conceals life
beautiful as the uprising of the poor
your face is delirious but I drink sanity in your eyes
your armpits are night but your breasts are day
your words are stone but your tongue is rain
your back is noon on the sea
your laughter is the sun buried in the suburbs
your hair unpinned is a storm on the terraces of dawn
your belly is the breath of the sea and the pulse of day
your name is downpour and your name is meadow
your name is high tide
you have all the names of water
But your sex is unnameable
the other face of being
the other face of time
the reverse of life
Here every speech ends
here beauty is illegible
here presence becomes awesome
folded into itself Presence is empty
the visible is invisible

Here the invisible becomes visible
here the star is black
light is shadow and shadow light
Here time stops
the four points of the compass meet
it is the lonely place and the meeting place

City Woman Presence
time ends here
here it begins

Beloved to love you

Beloved to love you as the marguerite awakening
furled corporeal among the black unwinged hoar-frosts
sometimes dead carried at the throat as a talisman
you raid your frontiers for the indulgence of earth
I take from your hand the white the lovely seed

As your breasts are suns glancing down your body
let us steal women's lips
let us fly together
and the lady flies far.

I disown in a calm voice between night and day
forever the love which does not abut
onto a clenched planet
The naming of you
of your pistils straying beyond my arms
of mallows which reign
anchored to the end of the bouquet gathering
that amorous waist
smile of the donjon

The boughs of your flesh fall again on the flagstone
animal at the diamond-panes and the earthed violet
when each northern stem is dead and the cloister
down there sustains its fruits of saltpeter and mango
closed eyes of the close woman
let us board these skiffs
and then downriver

and those eyes which lie
and lashes over such pools

Now is the red velvet night barns at the tropic beggarwoman begs
sign of the bell-clap the shrewish storm
there the bird struggles washed by hands of the rain
you so gentle at the window onto my headlong flight
adorned abandoned like a century gone

To the alcove of your tears
to your silken foot there the might of weapons far away
to my Spanish jennet
caparisoned with nerines with black stars and freesias.

Wink

Parakeets fly through my head when I see you in profile
and the greasy sky streaks with blue flashes
tracing your name in all directions
Rosa coiffed with a black tribe standing in rows on the stairs
where women's pointed breasts look out through men's eyes
Today I look out through your hair
Rosa of morning opal
and I wake through your sight
Rosa of armour
I think through your exploding breasts
Rosa of a pool the frogs turn green
and I sleep in your navel of Caspian sea
Rosa of honeysuckle in the general strike
and I'm lost in your milky way shoulders the comets made fecund
Rosa of jasmine in the night of washing
Rosa of haunted house
Rosa of black forest filled with in blue and green stamps
Rose of kite over a vacant lot where children are fighting
Rose of cigar smoke
Rose of seafoam made crystal
Rosa

Hello

My airplane in flames my castle flooded with Rhenish wine
my black iris ghetto my crystal ear
my rock hurtling down the cliff to smash the country policeman
my opal snail my air mosquito
my quilt of birds of paradise my hair of black foam
my tomb burst open my red grasshopper rain
my flying island my turquoise grape
my wreck of cars mad and careful my wild flowerbed
my pistil of dandelion projected in my eye
my tulip onion in the brain
my gazelle wandering off in some moviehouse
my casket of sun my volcano fruit
my laugh like a hidden pool where distraught prophets drown
my flood of blackcurrant my nightshade butterfly
my blue waterfall like a tidal wave making springtime
my coral revolver's mouth drawing me like the gleaming well
glassy as the mirror where you watch the hummingbirds of your gaze escaping
lost in a linen show framed with mummies
I love you

Do you know

My sandpaper head rubbing so long on a crystal glass
of your image like a bird a wild boar keeps from its first flight
is full of the seaspray of your eyes like two oranges not to be picked
your eyes like a split stone or a tree lightning-struck
just like the small heart I hold in my pocket
against a stove redder than a burning zeppelin
like an agave flower burst open
a red flag
more tattered than wind-swept hair
longing to caress you like a bird just born
and so blue you'd say a dead leaf greening
so shiny you'd say a wafer in a bath
where you'd seem just a water lily leaf in the woods
just a wild strawberry in an air chamber
just my life at the bend of the road

Benjamin Péret

Fountain

He is Rosa without Rosa
says the frost glad to chill the white wine
about to crash in the churches some Easter day
He is Rosa without Rosa
and when the mad bull of the great cataract invades me
under his raven wings chased from a thousand towers in ruin
what's the weather like
It's Rosa weather with a real Rosa sun
and I'm about to drink Rosa while eating Rosa
until I drowse off in a Rosa sleep
dressed in Rosa dreams
and Rosa dawn will wake me like a Rosa mushroom
with the image of Rosa surrounded by a Rosa halo

Her great thighs

Her great thighs
her hips
her buttocks
her arms
her calves
her hands
her eyes
her cheeks
her hair
her nose
her throat
her tears

the planets the wide curtains drawn and the transparent sky hidden behind
    the grill –
the oil lamps and the little bells of the sugared canaries between the figures –
the milk bowl of feathers, snatched from every laugh undressing the nude
    from the weight of the arms taken away from the blooms of the vegetable
    garden –
so many dead games hung from the branches of the meadow of the
    school pearled with song –
lake lured with blood and thistles
hollyhock played at gaming
needles of liquid shadow and bouquets of crystal algae open to dance steps
    the moving colours shakers at the bottom of the spilled-out glass –
to the lilac mask dressed with rain –

Philippe Soupault

Georgia

I'm not sleeping Georgia
I'm shooting arrows into the night Georgia
I'm awaiting Georgia
I'm thinking Georgia
The fire is like the snow Georgia
The night is my neighbour Georgia
I'm listening to every single sound Georgia
I see the smoke rising and flying off Georgia
I'm walking like a wolf in the shadow Georgia
I'm running here are the streets the suburbs Georgia
Here's a town which is the same
and that I don't know Georgia
I'm rushing here's the wind Georgia
and the cold and the silence and the fear Georgia
I'm fleeing Georgia
I'm running Georgia
the clouds are low they're about to fall Georgia
I stretch out my arms Georgia
I don't close my eyes Georgia
I call Georgia
I cry Georgia
I call Georgia
I call you Georgia
Will you come Georgia
soon Georgia
Georgia Georgia Georgia
Georgia

I'm not sleeping Georgia
I'm waiting for you
Georgia

Song for ghosts and for those now gone

Today there are hands I love,
Yesterday it was a nape
Tomorrow it will be lips
and this evening a smile
In three days a face
So each day in the week
I marvel at still living
Monday I may recall the way you walk
and Tuesday perhaps your hair
I'll also have to hear the voice
That of the ghosts
One hesitating one persuading
that life is not so terrible
as I thought it just now
Wednesday forget everything
But Thursday it's a perfume
you can't forget
the perfume of the rainbow
the other days
All the other days
I've promised not
to say nothing except to me

A recipe: how to produce erotic dreams

Ingredients: One kilo black radishes; three white hens; one
 head of garlic; four kilos honey; one mirror; two calf's livers;
 one brick; two clothespins; one whalebone corset; two false
 moustaches; two hats of your choice.
Pluck the hens, carefully setting aside the feathers. Boil in two
 quarts of unsalted distilled water or rainwater, along with
 the peeled, crushed garlic. Simmer on a low fire. While
 simmering, position the bed northwest to southeast and let
 it rest by an open window. After half an hour, close the
 window and place the red brick under the left leg at the
 head of the bed, which must face northwest, and let it rest.
While the bed rests, grate the black radishes directly over the
 consommé, taking special care to allow your hands to
 absorb the steam. Mix well and simmer. With a spatula,
 spread the four kilos of honey on the bedsheets and
 sprinkle the chicken-feathers on the honey-smeared
 sheets. Now, make the bed carefully.
The feathers do not all have to be white – they can be any
 colour, but be sure you avoid Guinea hen feathers, which
 sometimes provoke a state of prolonged nymphomania,
 or dangerous cases of priapism.
Put on corset, tighten well, and sit in front of the mirror. To
 relax your nerves, smile and try on the moustaches and
 hats, whichever you prefer (three-cornered Napoleonic,
 cardinal's hat, lace cap, Basque beret, etc.).
Put the two clothespins on a saucer and set it near the bed.
 Warm the calf's livers in a waterbath, but be careful not to

boil. Use the warm livers in place of a pillow (in cases of masochism) or on both sides of the bed, within reach (in cases of sadism).

From this moment on, everything must be done very quickly, to keep the livers from getting cold. Run and pour the broth (which should have a certain consistency) into a cup. As quickly as possible, return with it to the mirror, smile, take a sip of broth, try on one of the moustaches, take another sip, try on a hat, drink, try on everything, taking sips in between. Do all this as rapidly you possibly can.

When you have consumed all the broth, run to the bed and jump between the prepared sheets, quickly take the clothespins and put one on each big toe. These clothespins must be worn all night, firmly pressed to the nails, at a $45°$ angle from the toes.

This simple recipe guarantees good results, and normal people can proceed pleasantly from a kiss to strangulation, from rape to incest, etc., etc.

Recipes for more complicated cases, such as necrophilia, autophagia, tauromachia, romachia, alpinism, and others, can be found in a special volume in our collection of *Discreetly Healthy Advice*.

Louis Aragon

Paris 1897 – Paris 1982

Aragon founded the dada journal *Littérature* with Breton and Soupault in 1919. He joined the surrealist group in 1924, and remained a member until 1932. His first collections of poems were *Feu de joie* (Bonfire, 1920), and *Mouvement perpétuel* (Perpetual Motion, 1925). His prose works *Anicet; ou, le panorama* (Anicet; or, the Panorama, 1921), *Les Aventures de Télémaque* (The Adventures of Télémaque, 1923), *Le Paysan de Paris* (Paris Peasant, 1924), and *Traité du style* (Treatise on Style, 1928), are among the highlights of dada and surrealist writings. Reneging on many of the ideas he had earlier defended, Aragon left the surrealist group in 1932 on political grounds. He became a leading figure within the French Communist Party in the post-war period, acting as Director of the Maison de la Culture and editor of the newspaper *Ce Soir.*

André Breton

Tinchebray 1896 – Paris 1966

The charismatic leader of the surrealist movement, Breton became known, among friends and detractors alike, as 'the pope of surrealism'. Having trained as a doctor and worked with shell-shocked soldiers during the First World War, he was from the beginning interested in psychology and, in particular, in the theories of Sigmund Freud. Abandoning his medical career to concentrate on writing, he wrote with Philippe Soupault *Les Champs magnétiques* (Magnetic Fields, 1921). This was the first published example of surrealist automatic writing. Breton was the author of the manifesto that launched the movement in 1924. In this he declared that the aim of the movement was to reveal the 'real functioning of thought'. His novel *Nadja* (1928) was an exploration of the events and circumstances surrounding his short-lived love affair with a young woman of that name. In *Les Vases communicants* (Communicating Vessels, 1932), he wrote of the intermingling of dream and reality, and mused on the social conditions necessary for love to flourish. His lyric novel about surrealist love, *L'Amour fou* (Mad Love, 1937), celebrated his meeting with his second wife, the artist Jacqueline Lamba, and ended with the birth of their daughter Aube. During the Second World War, Breton left Paris, taking refuge in Marseilles. From there, he travelled to Martinique and on to New York. There he founded the journal *VVV* with Marcel Duchamp and the American painter David Hare, for whom Jacqueline left him. After the war, Breton and his new wife Elisa returned to France, where the surrealists regrouped. Breton continued to lead the surrealist group until his death in 1966.

Jacques-Bernard Brunius
Paris 1906 – Exeter 1967
Brunius began his career as a poet, later turning to film-making. He assisted Luis Buñuel in making the film *L'Age d'or* (The Golden Age, 1930), and went on to make short films under the direction of Jean Renoir. During the Second World War Brunius came to England where he became a key figure in the English surrealist group. He contributed to several anthologies and from London kept up his connections with the surrealist group in Paris.

Aimé Césaire
Basse-Pointe, Martinique 1913
Césaire was, alongside Léopold Sédar Senghor, the chief formulator of the concept of *négritude*, an influential movement that aimed to restore the cultural identity of black Africans. He studied in Paris, and in 1939 wrote his epic poem *Cahier d'un retour au pays natal* (Notebook of a Return to the Native Country). In Martinique he founded the journal *Tropiques*, and became both a teacher and a communist deputy in the

French National Assembly. In works such as *Les Armes miraculeuses* (Miraculous Weapons, 1946), he voiced rebellion in a European language dominated by African imagery. Eventually, he moved from *négritude* to black militism, and from poetry to political theatre.

René Char
L'Isle-sur-Sorgue 1907 – Paris 1988
Char joined the surrealist group in late 1929, and in 1930 edited with Breton and Eluard the collection of poems *Ralentir travaux* (Slow Works). He signed surrealist tracts, and published a number of volumes of his writings with the group's imprint, the Editions Surréalistes. *Artine* (1930) celebrates one of the most mysterious female figures in surrealist literature. According to Char, Artine had a dual origin: a young maid who came to work for Char's mother and died shortly afterwards, and a girl he met and kissed at a racetrack several years earlier. Although Char was to leave the surrealists and forge his own path, from 1933 much of his poetry bears the unmistakable mark of their approach. *Feuillets d'Hypnos* (Hypnos Waking, 1946) consists of pages from the notebook Char kept during his work in the resistance in the south of France. *Fureur et mystère* (Furor and

Mystery, 1948) and *Les Matinaux* (Those Who Rise Early, 1950) are among his best known volumes of poetry.

Salvador Dalí

Figueres, Spain 1904 – Figueres, Spain 1989
Dalí was a flamboyant artist, known almost as much for his eccentric behaviour as for his meticulously executed paintings of obsessions and fantasies. He collaborated with his friend Luis Buñuel on the scripts for the classic surrealist films *Un chien andalou* (Andalusian Dog, 1928), and *L'Age d'or* (The Golden Age, 1930). In 1929 he was enthusiastically received by the Paris-based surrealist group, and his approach to art had a decisive impact on the development of the movement. However, his unwillingness to follow the leadership of Breton, and, above all, his support in the late 1930s for the Spanish fascist dictator General Franco, led to his expulsion from the movement. In his scandalous and brilliant autobiography *The Secret Life of Salvador Dalí*, published in 1942, Dalí revealed much about the complexes that fuelled his art and the influence his wife, Gala, had had on his life. As an expression of his love for her, and of his identification with her, he signed many of his canvases Gala Dalí.

Léon-Gontran Damas

Guyana 1912 – 1978
Damas made contact with Césaire and Senghor in Paris in the 1930s, becoming an adherent of *négritude*. He published an autobiographical work, *Return to Guyana*, in 1938. Later anthologies of his verse include *Black Label* (1956), and *Pigments* (1960). *African Songs of Love, War, Grief and Abuse* (1961) portrays Guyanese village life.

Robert Desnos

Paris 1900 – Terezina, Czechoslovakia 1945
Desnos came into contact with the surrealists in the early 1920s. He experimented with automatic writing, and was able to utter poetic pronouncements while in states of 'hypnotic sleep'. In 1924 he used automatic writing in *Deuil pour deuil* (Mourning for Mourning), a prose poem of novella length. He had long been interested in the subject of erotic literature and in 1927 certain pages of his *La Liberté ou l'amour!* (Freedom or Love!) were censored because of their strong erotic content. This work, and the earlier 'Poèmes à la mystérieuse', were inspired by his love for a music-hall singer, Yvonne Georges. Through the 1920s and beyond Desnos supported himself as a journalist, which brought him into conflict with the surrealists' views on work; and, for

his part, he disapproved of the surrealists' support of communism. Unsurprisingly, he left the group in 1928, a move that coincided with his meeting of his future wife Youki. In 1944 he was arrested by the Gestapo and deported. He died of typhus in the concentration camp of Terezina.

Paul Eluard

Saint-Denis 1895 – Charenton-le-pont 1952
One of the most important lyrical poets of the twentieth century, Eluard played a key role in the development of surrealism. While still a teenager he married the young Russian Helena Dimitrovnie Diakonova, who he nicknamed Gala. He considered Gala as the love of his life, notwithstanding their various affairs, until it became clear that her relationship with the painter Dalí was permanent. For her he wrote the great love poems gathered in *Au Défaut du silence* (In the Absence of Silence, 1925), *Capitale de la douleur* (Capital of Pain, 1926), and *L'Amour, la poésie* (Love, Poetry, 1929). In 1930 he met Maria Benz, known as Nusch, for whom he wrote *La Vie immédiate* (Immediate Life, 1932), *Comme deux gouttes d'eau* (Like Two Peas in a Pod, 1933), and *Facile* (Easy, 1935). Eluard had been perhaps Breton's closest friend within the group, but when, in 1938, Eluard chose to give his allegiance to the

Communist Party, against the stated position of the surrealist group, Breton broke with him. Although after the war they both lived in Paris, they were never to meet again.

Marcelle Ferry

1904–1984
Ferry – who was known as 'Lila' – joined the surrealist group in Paris in 1932. Her collection of poems *L'Isle d'un jour* (The Daylong Island) was illustrated by Yves Tanguy and published by Editions Surrèalistes in 1938. She had a short liaison with Breton, and a relationship with Georges Hugnet. The surrealist painter Oscar Dominguez was also her lover. She married Jean Lévy who took her surname and, as Jean Ferry, had success as a writer with *The Mechanic and Other Stories* (1953) and *Study of Raymond Roussel* (1953).

Frida Kahlo

Coyocán, Mexico 1907 – 1954
Aged six, Kahlo became a victim of polio, and, aged eighteen, suffered a catastrophic accident, involving a tram, which broke her spine. The pitiful condition of her body was the subject of many of her paintings, and of her vivid diary, published after her death. She married the Mexican muralist Diego Rivera in 1929, and both received Breton

when he visited Mexico in 1938. Breton was enamoured of Kahlo's work and personality, but she remained privately contemptuous of the surrealist group. Nonetheless, she exhibited in the international surrealist exhibition in Mexico City in 1940, participated in the activities of the surrealist group in Mexico, and explored dream imagery and automatism in her writings. She was particularly close to Jacqueline Lamba, Breton's second wife.

Annie Le Brun
Rennes 1942
Le Brun was a member of the surrealist group in Paris from 1963, and was, with the poet Radovan Ivsic, close to Breton until his death. No-one better represents the living spirit of surrealism than these two with their uncompromising loyalty to the movement as they knew it. One of the last books produced under the imprint Editions Surréalistes, Le Brun's *Sur-le-Champ* (Right Now, 1967), was illustrated by the Czech painter Toyen. It was followed by *Lâchez tout* (Drop Everything, 1977). *Les Châteaux de la Subversion* (Castles of Subversion, 1982) concerned the Gothic novel and addressed the relationship between the imagination and revolutionary desire. Le Brun edited the complete works of the Marquis de Sade and those of Raymond Roussel, and is known for her polemical and revolutionary texts, including *Pour Aimé Césaire* (For Aimé Césaire, 1994).

Gilbert Lély
Paris 1904 – Paris 1984
A close friend of René Char from 1934 to 1947, Lély is known as the biographer and editor of the writings of the Marquis de Sade and as a fervent defender of the sexual impulse in all its revolutionary manifestations. His books include: *Allusions ou poèmes* (Allusions or Poems, 1927); *Ne tue ton père qu'au bon escient* (Only Kill Your Father If You Know What You Are Doing, 1932); *Je ne veux pas qu'on tue cette femme* (I Don't Want That Woman Killed, 1936); *Ma Civilisation* (My Civilisation, 1942); and *L'Inceste d'été* (Summer Incest, 1964).

Dora Maar
Paris 1907 – Paris 1997
After living for a period in Buenos Aires, Maar returned to Paris with her family and studied at various art schools. She met Jacqueline Lamba, who was to become Breton's second wife, and with whom she was to remain close friends. A photographer and a painter, she participated in many

surrealist exhibitions; the D for Dora in the middle of the name of the surrealist art gallery 'Gradiva', was inspired by her. She wrote poems from an early date, before her celebrated relationship with Picasso, which lasted from 1936 to 1942. She was to continue writing poetry after the ending of the affair, until her death as a recluse in 1997.

Joyce Mansour
Bowden, England 1928 – Paris 1986
Born of Egyptian parents, Mansour was educated in Switzerland, and moved to Paris in 1953. Her volume of poems *Cris* (Cries, 1953) was instantly acclaimed by the surrealist group. Her writings were characterized by an eroticism that embraced both humour and a concern with death. Other volumes include *Déchirures* (Tearings Apart, 1955), and *Rapaces* (Rapacious, 1960). She also wrote a number of important prose and theatre pieces, and her texts were illustrated by such artists as Alechinsky, Lam and Matta.

Maria
Campanha, Brazil 1900–1973
In the 1940s Maria Martins led something of a double life. In one role, she was the charming and vivacious wife of the Brazilian ambassador to the United States, based in Washington D.C. In the other role, in which she was known publicly simply as Maria, she was a successful sculptor, whose works were bought by many leading institutions in America. Her style evolved from a Gauguinesque exoticism to a less naturalistic, and more emotionally charged, style in the early 1940s, as she mixed with the émigré surrealists in New York. In the mid-1940s she became the lover of the artist Marcel Duchamp, and her works of this period reflect something of the intensity of their relationship. Maria exhibited at the international surrealist exhibitions in Paris in 1947 and in 1959, and Breton wrote an appreciative text about her work.

Alice Paalen
Chenecey-Buillon, Doubs 1904 – Mexico 1987
Alice Rahon married the painter Wolfgang Paalen in 1934. Hard hit by the end of her short-lived affair with Picasso, she joined the poet Valentine Penrose in India where the two women lived together. In 1936 she published a volume of poems *A même la terre* (Even the Earth) with the Editions Surréalistes. In 1939 she went with Wolfgang Paalen to Mexico. Although he publicly (albeit temporarily) broke with surrealism, she continued to defend its precepts throughout her life.

Octavio Paz
Mexico 1914 – Mexico 1998
One of the major Latin American writers of the twentieth century, Paz published his first book of poetry *Luna silvestre* (Forest Moon) in 1933 at the age of nineteen. In 1937 he joined the Spanish Republican army, and contacted the surrealists in Paris before returning home. In Mexico he founded several literary reviews. His major poetic publications included *No Pasaran!* (They Shall Not Pass, 1937), *Aguila o sol?* (Eagle or Sun?, 1951), and *Piedra de sol* (The Sun Stone, 1957). Between 1946 and 1950 he was the cultural attaché to the Mexican Embassy in Paris, where he maintained his contact with the surrealist group. Paz received the Nobel Prize for literature in 1990.

Valentine Penrose
Mont-de-Marsan 1903 – Chiddingly, England 1978
In 1925 Valentine Boué married the British painter Roland Penrose. He was close to the French surrealists, and she moved within their circle without officially joining the movement. She contributed to the surrealist survey on love, and her first collection of poems *Herbe à la Lune* (Grass on the Moon) was published in 1935, with a preface by Paul Eluard. She traveled to

Spain in 1936 to support the workers in their fight against the fascists, and during the Second World War served in the French Resistance. In 1951 she published *Dons de Féminins* (Feminine Gifts), a cycle of poems and collages. A selection of her poems and other writings, *Poems and Narrations*, was published in English in 1976.

Benjamin Péret
Rézé 1899 – Paris 1959
Poet and political militant, Péret was a member of the Parisian dada group and a co-founder of surrealism. He joined the Communist Party in 1925, and from the early 1930s tended towards Trotskyism. During the Spanish Civil War he traveled to Spain to assist the republican cause, and there met his future wife, the painter Remedios Varo. Following the fall of France, they went to Mexico, where they formed the nucleus of a surrealist group until 1947 when Péret returned to Paris. One of the most faithful adherents of the group, Péret was a close friend of Breton, and shared his vision of ideal love as elective and reciprocal. His most famous volumes of poetry include *Le Grand jeu* (The Great Game, 1928), *De Derrière les fagots* (From the Hidden Store, 1934), and *Je sublime* (I Sublimate/Sublime Game, 1936).

Pablo Picasso

Malaga 1888 – Mougins 1973
A giant of twentieth-century painting, Picasso explored many forms and styles of expression throughout his long career. In the early 1940s he wrote surrealist poems, under the influence of Breton, and in collaboration with his companion, the photographer Dora Maar. His surrealist play, *Le Désir attrapé par la queue* (Desire Caught by the Tail), written in 1941, received its debut in 1944 in the apartment of Michel and Louise Leiris, acted a cast of actors that included the Leirises, Dora Maar, Sartre and Simone de Beauvoir. Breaking rules of syntax and dispensing with logic, Picasso's poetic writings can be seen as examples of surrealist automatic writing.

Philippe Soupault

Chaville 1897 – Paris 1990
Soupault, with Breton and Aragon, was one of the main figures in the Parisian dada movement. With Breton, he edited the dada journal *Littérature*, and wrote *Les Champs magnétiques* (Magentic Fields, 1919). However, his independent line in matters relating to his work for newspapers and to politics (he opposed the group's adhesion to the Communist party) led to his expulsion from the surrealist group in 1926.

Georgia (1925) contains some of his most lyric writing. Other poetic works include *Aquarium* (1917) and *Rose des vents* (Rose of the winds, 1920). He also wrote the novel *Les Dernières Nuits de Paris* (Last Nights of Paris, 1928).

Remedios Varo

Anglès, Catalonia 1913 – Mexico 1963
Varo studied in Madrid and moved to Barcelona in 1935. She met Benjamen Péret, with whose militant Trotskyism she was in total agreement, and moved to Paris with him. There they were both committed members of the surrealist group. In 1942 they moved to Mexico, where they were active in the surrealist community, with the painter Leonora Carrington, the poet Octavio Paz and others. Varo participated in the international surrealist exhibitions in Paris (1938), Mexico (1940), and Paris (1947). When Péret returned to Paris in 1947, she remained in Mexico, and later married Walter Gruen. *De Homo Rodans*, a fine example of surrealist black humour, was published after her death in 1970.

Sources

Every effort has been made to trace the copyright holders of the poems included in this collection. The publishers apologise for any omissions that may inadvertently have been made.

All poems are translated by Mary Ann Caws unless otherwise stated.

Louis Aragon
p.22: From *Le Mouvement perpétuel*, Les Cahiers libres, Paris 1925
p.23: © Jean Ristat

André Breton
p.26: Trans. Mary Ann Caws and Patricia Terry. From 'Union Libre', 1931, in *Le Revolver à cheveux blancs*, © Editions Gallimard, Paris 1948
pp.28–35: From *L'Air de l'eau*, © Editions Gallimard, Paris 1948
p.36: From *Oubliés*, © Editions Gallimard, Paris 1948

Jacques-Bernard Brunius
p.38: From *Fulcrum*, Paris 1944

Aimé Césaire
p.40: From *Les Armes miraculeuses*, © Editions Gallimard, Paris 1946

René Char
p.41–4: From *Le marteau sans maître*, © Editions Surréalistes José Corti, Paris 1934

Salvador Dalí
p.48: Trans. Julian Levy, in Julian Levy (ed.), *Surrealism* © 1936 by The Black Sun Press, New York

Léon-Gontran Damas
p.50: From *Pigment névralgique*, Présence africaine, Paris 1972

Robert Desnos
pp.51–8: From 'A la mystérieuse', 1926, in *Corps et biens*, © Editions Gallimard, Paris 1930
pp.59–64: From 'Les Ténèbres', 1927, in *Corps*

et biens, © Editions Gallimard, Paris 1930

Paul Eluard
p.65–6: From 'Noveaux Poèmes', in *Capitale de la douleur*, © Editions Gallimard, Paris 1926
p.67: From *Le Phénix*, © Editions Seghers, Paris 1951
p.68–70: From 'Premièrement', in *L'amour, la poésie*, © Editions Gallimard, Paris 1929
p.72: From 'Mourir de ne pas mourir', in *Capitale de la douleur*, © Editions Gallimard, Paris 1926
pp.73–4: From *Corps mémorable*, © Editions Seghers, Paris 1947, 1996
p.75: From *Les temps déborde*, © Editions Seghers, Paris 1947

Marcelle Ferry
p.76: From *I'Isle d'un jour*, Editions Surrèalistes, Paris 1938. Trans. by Myrna Bell Rochester, in Penelope Rosemont (ed.), *Surrealist*

Women: An International Anthology, University of Texas, Austin 1998, pp.99–100

Frida Kahlo
Trans. from the Spanish by Hayden Herrera. In Rosemont 1998, pp. 145–6

Annie Le Brun
p.77: From 'Sur-le-Champ', *Tout Près, Les Nomades*, Paris 1967

Gilbert Lély
p.81: Source unknown. In Jean-Louis Gabin (ed.), *Poésies complètes*, Mercure de France, Paris 1990

Dora Maar
p.82: From a manuscript *c.*1942–3, in Mary Ann Caws, *Dora Maar With and Without Picasso: A Biography*, Thames and Hudson, London 2000, p.177.

Maria
p.90: From an undated manuscript, *c.*1940s, in *The*

Surrealist Sculptures of Maria Martins, exh. cat., Andre Emmerich Gallery, New York 1998, pp.22–3 (trans. not given)

Joyce Mansour
pp.83–5: From *Cris*, © Editions Seghers, Paris 1953
pp.86–9: From *Déchirures*, Editions de Minuit, Paris 1955.

Alice Paalen
p.91: From *Noir Animal*, Editions Dolores La Rue, Mexico 1941
p. 92: From *A Même la terre*, Editions Surrèalistes, Paris 1936

Octavio Paz
p.94: From *Salamander*, 1958–61, in *Octavio Paz, Collected Poems 1957–1987*, Carcanet Press and Elephant Trust, London 1998, p.101. Trans. Eliot Weinberger

Valentine Penrose
In Valentine Penrose, *Poems and Narrations*, Carcanet

Press and Elephant Trust, London 1977, pp.50–1. Trans. Roy Edwards

Benjamin Péret
pp.99–102: *Je sublime*, © Editions Surréalistes Jose Corti, Paris 1936.

Pablo Picasso
In Caws 2000, p.96

Philippe Soupault
p.104: Trans. Mary Ann Caws and Patricia Terry. From *Georgia*, Les Cahiers libres, Paris 1926
p.107: From 'Crépuscules', 1960–1967, in *Poèmes et poésies: 1917–1973*, Grasset, Paris 1974

Remedios Varo
p.108: From *De Homo Rodans*, Calli-Nova, Mexico City 1970, in Rosemont 1998, pp.280–2. Trans. from the Spanish by Walter Gruen